Hidden Pictures®

Marcos is having a blast water-skiing. Can you find the hidden objects in this scene?

Illustrated by Mike Dammer

balloon

mitten

toothbrush

comb

crown

dog bone

fishhook

pencil

sock

teacup

bell

ladle

carrot

slice of pie

Top This!

What do you like on your pizza? We've tossed **18** toppings into the grid. They are hidden up, down, across, backwards, and diagonally. Get them while they're hot!

```
              G O O
            E C I L S
          P I N E A P P L E   L
        L E S P I N A C H B J
      S P J N E K C I H C H
    E H P S M O O R H S U M R
    G R E E N P E P P E R S M
  T A I R T S V V D E L E L H Y
  O S M O O E G A R L I C S Y U
  H U P N M I S E V I L O W E M
    A F I A V B R O C C O L I
    S E S T O C A E G N M Y D
      E Q O H A M C I V K D
        B B E C V A O O Z N C
          A S N Q N B E N O
              A S P I E
              E A T
```

Posing for a Portrait

Compare these two pictures. Can you find at least **12** differences?

What a Trip!

Uncle Dexter is always traveling the globe, looking for adventure.
This time he's on a safari in Kenya. He just e-mailed you a photo from his wild day.
What do you think the picture shows? Draw Uncle Dexter's photo here.

Illustrated by Mike Moran

Ant Eater

Can you help this ant find its way to the food? Just one path will take it there.
Try not to get too antsy along the way!

Pen Pals

Get ready for a stu**PEN**dous puzzle. Use the clues below to fill in the answer spaces. Each answer includes the letters **P-E-N**. We're de**PEN**ding on you to fill in as many as you can.

1. Opposite of shut   <u>O</u> P E N

2. One cent   P E N __ __

3. To use your money   __ P E N __

4. Type of tree   __ __ P E N

5. It has an eraser.   P E N __ __ __

6. Flightless bird   P E N __ __ __ __

7. Where hogs live   __ __ __ __ P E N

8. Pitchers warm up here.   __ __ __ __ __ P E N

9. Another word for snake   __ __ __ __ P E N __

10. A punishment in hockey   P E N __ __ __ __ __

11. Shape with five sides   P E N __ __ __ __ __

12. Costs a lot   __ __ P E N __ __ __ __

13. A woodworker   __ __ __ P E N __ __ __

14. Hot pepper   __ __ __ __ __ P E Ñ __

15. The Fourth of July   __ __ __ __ __ P E N __ __ __ __ __

       __ __ __

Puzzle by Lori Mortensen

Illustrated by Kelly Kennedy

1. OPEN
2. PENNY
3. SPEND
4. ASPEN
5. PENCIL
6. PENGUIN
7. PIGPEN
8. BULLPEN
9. SERPENT
10. PENALTY
11. PENTAGON
12. EXPENSIVE
13. CARPENTER
14. JALAPEÑO
15. INDEPENDENCE DAY

Tic Tac Monster

What do the monsters in each row (horizontally, vertically, and diagonally) have in common?

Illustrated by Dave Clegg

What do you call a clean, neat, hardworking, kind monster?
A failure.

What do you do with a green monster?
Wait until it ripens.

What's the best way to talk to a monster?
Long distance.

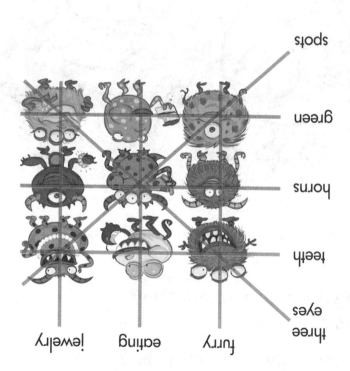

spots

green

horns

teeth

three
eyes

jewelry

eating

furry

Brain Games

START HERE
Take your brain on a hike.
How far can you go?

Name three places where you can see a star.

What is rhythm?

BFF **RSVP** **A.M.** **P.M.**
How many common abbreviations can you name?

Do all plants need the same things to survive? How do you know?

What makes something look tasty to you?

What do people do with their hands when they feel nervous? Thoughtful? Excited?

How is jumping with a jump rope different from jumping without one?

What is the best family memory you have?

What would it be like if everyone's clothing had bells attached?

Cool
POP 2,520   ELEV 1,518

If you could rename where you live, what would you call it?

THE END

What is your favorite thing about a newspaper?

How do you like to celebrate your birthday?

Illustrated by Erin Mauterer

Rhyme Time

At the Sillyville Flea Market, there's a star in a jar, a stork with a fork, and a bent tent!
What other rhyming things do you see?

Illustrated by Neil Numberman

We found these rhymes. You may have found others! bent/tent, pug/rug, squirrel/pearl, lizard/wizard, llamas/pajamas, goat/coat, sheep/jeep, doll/shawl, stamp/lamp, Great Dane/train/plane, fish/dish, duck/puck, wombat/flat/hat, cat/bat, mouse/blouse, frog/log, star/jar, kittens/mittens, bear/chair, cricket/ticket, jacket/racket, stork/fork, raccoon/balloon, baboon/bassoon, chick/stick, fox/socks

Hidden Words

There are **6** words (not pictures!) hidden in the scene below.
Can you find **BALLOON**, **CAKE**, **FRIENDS**, **GAMES**, **GIFT**, and **PARTY**?

Illustrated by Dave Klug

 TONGUE TWISTERS
Say each one three times fast!

Brad blew up a blue balloon.
Piper prepped the party plates.
Greg gave Gavin a green gift.

What's Wrong?

Which things in this picture are silly? It's up to you!

Step by Step

Follow the steps to draw a castle or draw one from your own head.

1.

2.

3.

4.

5.

Illustrated by Ron Zalme

Hidden Pictures®

Check out all the great books at this library! Can you find the hidden objects in this scene?

artist's brush

crescent moon

spoon

party hat

carrot

pizza

ruler

belt

heart

baseball bat

worm

crown

toothbrush

scissors

Back to the Drawing Board

Are you feeling crafty? We've gathered **16** arts and crafts supplies for you. Their names fit into the grid in just one way. Use the number of letters in each word as a clue to where it might fit.

4 Letters
CLAY
FELT
GLUE
YARN

5 Letters
BEADS
PAPER
RULER

6 Letters
CANVAS
ERASER
PAINTS

7 Letters
BRUSHES
~~CRAYONS~~
GLITTER
MARKERS
PASTELS

8 Letters
SCISSORS

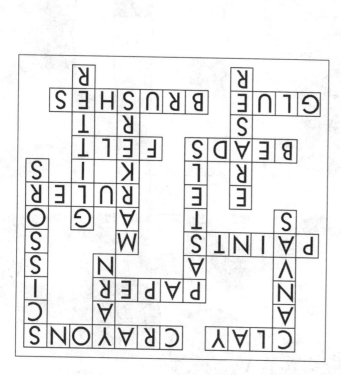

Comic Relief

Compare these two pictures. Can you find at least **12** differences?

Illustrated by Mike Dammer

Thinking Cap

Professor Anita Brainstorm is trying out her latest invention, the Supersonic
Super-Duper Thinking Cap. What do you think the professor is thinking about right now?
Use your imagination and draw it in before her brainwaves crash!

Construction Conundrum

Find your way from START to FINISH. Then solve the puzzle below.

START

FINISH

Illustrated by Dave Klug

Benny Cook works on this construction site. He likes certain things. What do they have in common?

- He drives the bulldozer but not the forklift.
- He eats egg-and-cheese tortillas for lunch but never soup.
- On his break he does crossword puzzles but not word searches.
- He tells riddles but not jokes.
- He commutes in a carpool but doesn't take the bus.

Benny likes things with double letters.

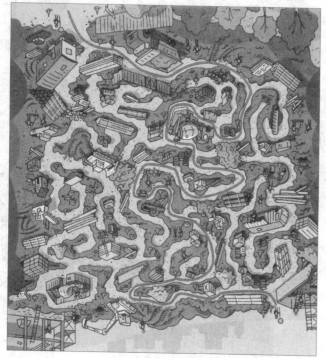

Work It Out

To "work out" the answer to the riddle below, first cross out all the pairs of matching letters.
Then write the remaining letters in order in the spaces next to the riddle.

QQ EE BB JU MM OO WW
LL MP SS VV YY ZZ IN
II AA RR NN EE GF YY
HH XX PP DD LA UU SS
GG OO PJ SS CC QQ II
CC YY EE MM AA TT AC
UU BB KK VV ZZ KS TT

What kind of
exercises do
pancakes do?

_ _ _ _ _ _ _ _

_ _ _ _ _ _ _ _

Illustrated by Dan McGeehan

What kind of exercises do pancakes do?
JUMPING FLAPJACKS

Tic Tac Superhero

What do the superheroes in each row (horizontally, vertically, and diagonally) have in common?

Illustrated by Dave Clegg

Why did the superhero save the pickle?
Because he wanted to eat it later.

Where do superheroes shop?
At the supermarket.

What's the difference between a superhero and a fly?
A superhero can fly, but a fly can't superhero.

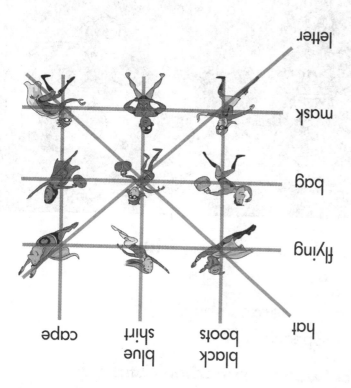

Brain Games

Take your brain on a hike. How far can you go?

START

Name a few fruits in order of their juiciness.

What is the **FUNNIEST** song you know?

Name five places that you'd like to EXPLORE.

What do **DANCING**

and

PAINTING

have in common?

"My home is like a . . ." How would you finish that sentence?

Name three foods that you **WOULD NOT** put on a snack cracker.

What is the best thing someone has taught you?

WITHOUT MOVING YOUR HANDS, explain how to open a jar.

Why do you think spoons are curved instead of shaped like a box?

THE END

What do you do for fun that uses your **IMAGINATION?**

What does it mean to say that someone **STUMBLES UPON AN IDEA?**

Illustrated by Erin Mauterer

Bird Buddies

Each bird on the top wire has a twin below with the same coloring.
Can you find each twin?

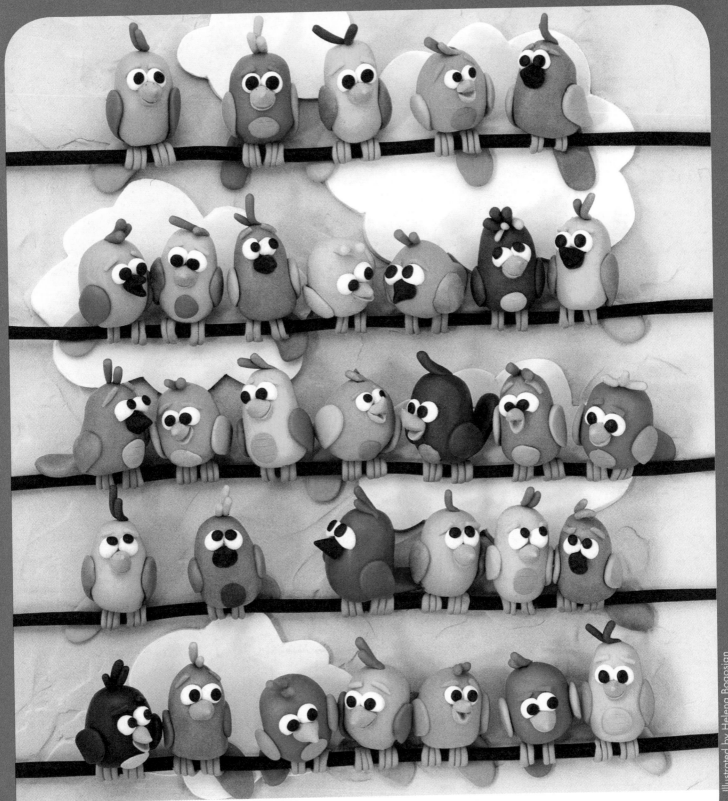

Illustrated by Helena Bogosian

BONUS!
What do the birds on each wire have in common? For example, the birds on the top wire all have their tails down.

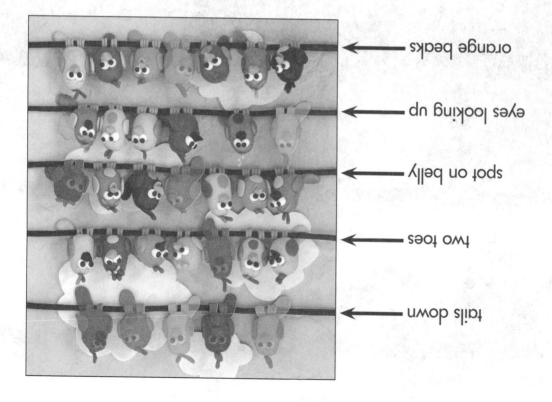

← orange beaks

← eyes looking up

← spot on belly

← two toes

← tails down

Map Mix-Up

People are flocking to Logicville for the big Summer Festival. Unfortunately, the new town maps were printed without labels on most of the buildings on Main Street. To help the lost tourists, read the clues below to figure out which building is which. Fill in the correct names on the map.

1. Archie's Arcade is one building south of the Sandwich Hut.

2. Izzy's Ice Cream is northeast of Archie's Arcade.

3. The Movie Palace is north of Sim's Sweets.

4. The T-Shirt Shack is one building south of Izzy's.

Illustrated by Garry Colby   Puzzle by Sara Matson

Movie Palace   Sandwich Hut   Izzy's Ice Cream

Sim's Sweets   Archie's Arcade   T-Shirt Shack

What's Wrong?®

Which things in this picture are silly? It's up to you!

Illustrated by Gary LaCoste

Just Sayin'...

Give this robot something to say. Then find the hidden canoe, flashlight, pliers, screw, and screwdriver.

Illustrated by Bill Basso

Hidden Pictures®

The Garcias are picking veggies from their garden. Can you find the hidden objects in this scene?

Illustrated by Mike Moran

t-shirt

mailbox

magic wand

present

teacup

drinking straw

pennant

necktie

hockey stick

ruler

magnet

party hat

slipper

belt

Worm Search

Twenty kinds of worms have wiggled into this grid. They are hiding up, down, across, backwards, and diagonally. We circled FIELD. Can you unearth the rest?

Word List

- ~~FIELD~~
- **FIRE**
- **FLAT**
- **FLUKE**
- **GLOW**
- **HEART**
- **HOOK**
- **INCH**
- **MEAL**
- **NIGHTCRAWLER**
- **RED WIGGLER**
- **ROUND**
- **SEA**
- **SILK**
- **SPAGHETTI**
- **TAPE**
- **THREAD**
- **TUBE**
- **WAX**
- **WHIP**

Puzzle by Lori Mortensen

Illustrated by Jim Steck

```
N I G H T C R A W L E R
S P A G H E T T I S D M
P X A W I N C H P R A R
F L U K E M H O O K E E
I R P E D R E C G Y R D
E Z V W N O A Q P I H W
I R Z S U W R Y M W T I
V I I L O K T H O E D G
X L C F R O W L V M A G
K T A P E O G F L A T L
D L E I F B U N B E S E
J E S T U B E P Q X Q R
```

BONUS PUZZLE

The smartest worm of all is hiding somewhere in the grid. Dig deep and see if you can find it.

Space Encounter

Compare these two pictures. Can you find at least **12** differences?

Illustrated by Kevin Zimmer

The Hole Story

What a find! Doug just dug up something completely unexpected.
What do you think he discovered? Draw it here.

Illustrated by Mike Moran

Waterslide Splash

Today is a grrrr-8 day to visit the water park! These bears took a ride on the slide.
Figure out which of them can make it to FINISH. Then see how many 8's you can find in the scene.

Country Sudoku

Grab your passport—we're heading around the world! Each grid holds one country. Fill in the boxes so that each row, column, and six-letter section contains the letters of that country. We've filled in some of the letters to get you started. Can you fill in the rest?

FRANCE grid:

F	R	A	N	C	E
		C	A		R
R			C	N	
N	C			E	A
			R	A	N
		R	N	F	

TURKEY grid:

T	U	R	K	E	Y
E					
	E		T		
	R	T	E		R
Y					
R			Y	U	K

BRAZIL grid:

B	R	A	Z	I	L
Z					B
	B	I			
			R	Z	A
I	L	R			I
A	B		L		
	I		A	B	Z

F	R	A	N	C	E
E	N	C	A	F	R
R	A	E	C	N	F
N	C	F	R	E	A
C	F	R	E	A	N
A	E	N	F	R	C

T	U	R	K	E	Y
E	Y	K	U	R	T
U	E	Y	T	K	R
K	R	T	E	Y	U
Y	K	U	R	T	E
R	T	E	Y	U	K

B	R	A	Z	I	L
L	Z	I	R	A	B
Z	A	B	I	L	R
I	L	R	B	Z	A
A	B	Z	L	R	I
R	I	L	A	B	Z

Tic Tac Pizza

What do the pizzas in each row (horizontally, vertically, and diagonally) have in common?

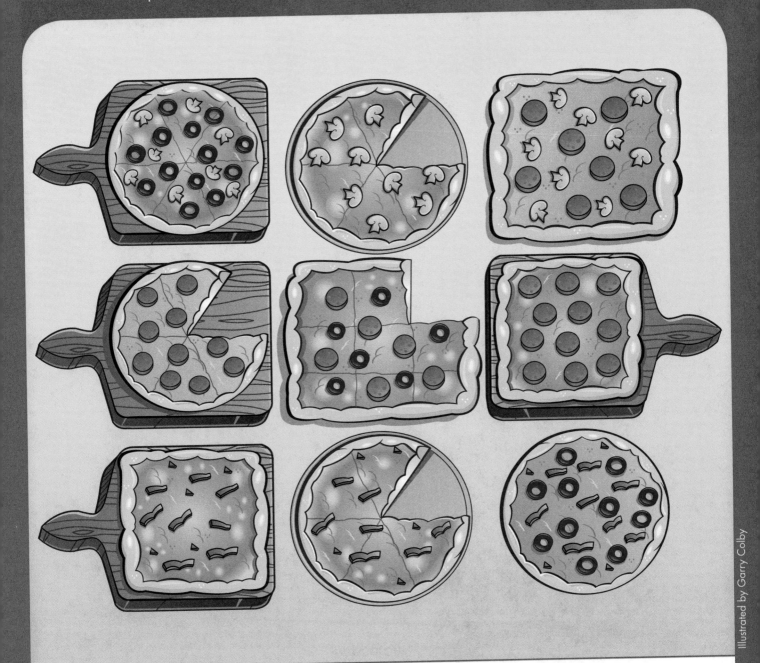

How do you fix a broken pizza?
With tomato paste.

What topping do teachers put on their pizza?
Graded cheese.

Knock, knock.
Who's there?
Sharon.
Sharon who?
You Sharon that pizza with me, or what?

Illustrated by Garry Colby

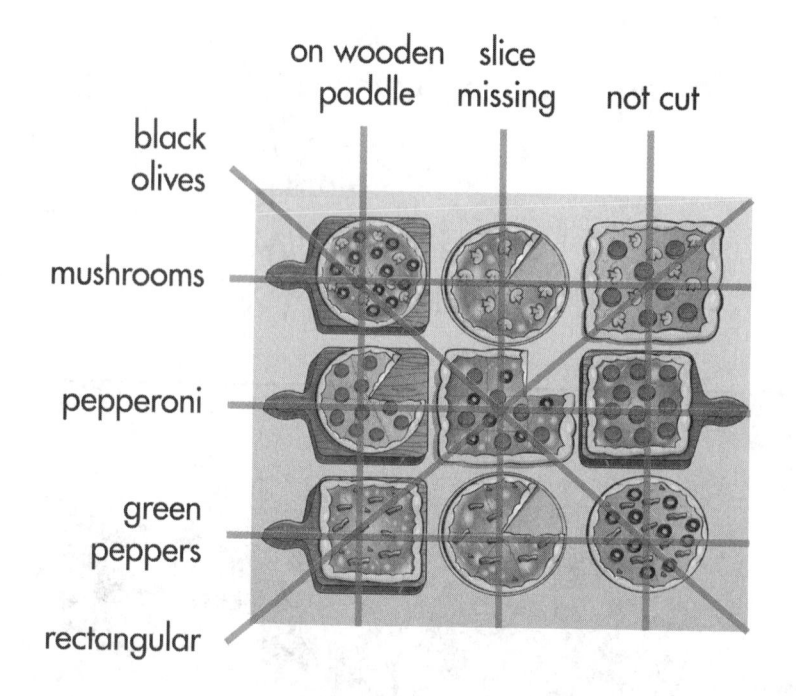

Brain Games

START
Take your brain on a hike. How far can you go?

Name five sounds you hear in the summer.

What is the best thing in your closet? Why?

Why don't most hats **HAVE POCKETS?**

DON'T FORGET

What would it be like if people could remember everything?

Name three things that look the same if they are **flipped over.**

Which do you like better, **A BEANBAG CHAIR** **OR** **A ROCKING CHAIR?**

What are some words that affect HOW YOU FEEL?

If your water bottle sprang a leak, how would you keep the water from coming out?

THE END

What would **NOT** make a good bookmark?

How can fear hurt you?

Do you have to think about being kind, or does it just happen?

If you could own a copy of just one story, what would it be?

How can fear help you?

Illustrated by Erin Mauterer

Band Together

The Critterville Community Band hits all the right notes—and hides others!
Can you find **18** eighth notes ♪ hidden here?

Illustrated by Rocky Fuller

BONUS!
Alligator starts with **A**. Can you find items in this scene that start with the other letters of the alphabet?

BONUS: We found these items. You may have found others! alligator, bear, cymbals, dog, eagle, flute, giraffe, harmonica, iguana, juice box, koala, lion, mouse, necklace, opossum, pig, quail, raccoon, saxophone, tuba, ukulele, violin, walrus, xylophone, yak, zebra

Hidden Words

There are six words (not pictures!) hidden in the scene below.
Can you find **CANDY**, **GAMES**, **PRIZE**, **RIDE**, **TICKETS**, and **WIN**?

Illustrated by Kelly Kennedy

TONGUE TWISTERS
Say each one three times fast!

Regular roller-coaster riders ride right up front.
Paul picked a particular prize.
Cotton candy can be crunchy.

What's Wrong?

Which things in this picture are silly? It's up to you!

EAT AT JOE'S

Illustrated by Neil Numberman

Step by Step

Follow the steps to draw a guitar or draw one from your own head.

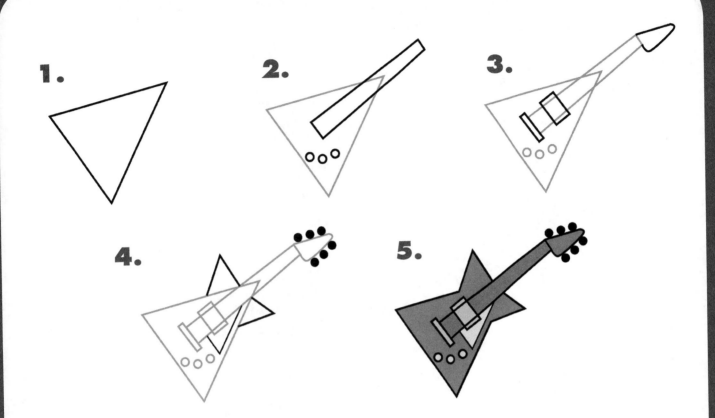

1.

2.

3.

4.

5.

Hidden Pictures®

Something's fishy in this aquarium. Can you find the hidden objects in this scene?

Illustrated by Kevin Zimmer

button   paper clip   banana   baby's rattle   bowling pin   magnet   slice of pizza   wedge of orange

golf club   waffle cone   leaf   magnifying glass   fork   eyeglasses   key   bowling ball   feather   toothbrush

What's on the Menu?

¡Hola! We're serving up **18** items that you might order at a Mexican restaurant. Each of these foods can fit into the grid in just one way. Use the number of letters in each word as a clue to where it might fit. Go ahead and dig in!

MENU

~~BEANS~~
BURRITO
CARNITAS
CHILI
CHIMICHANGA
CHIPS
ENCHILADA
FAJITA
GORDITA

GUACAMOLE
QUESADILLA
RICE
SALAD
SALSA
TACO
TAMALE
TAQUITO
TORTA

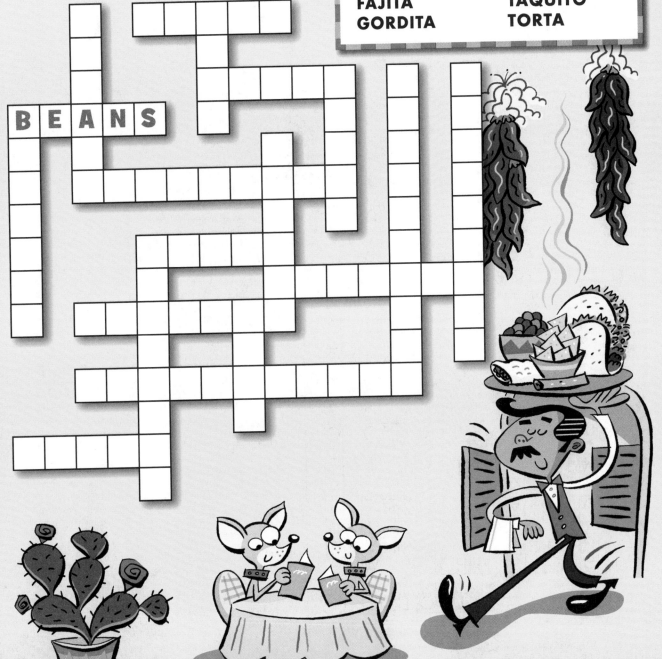

BEANS

Illustrated by Kelly Kennedy

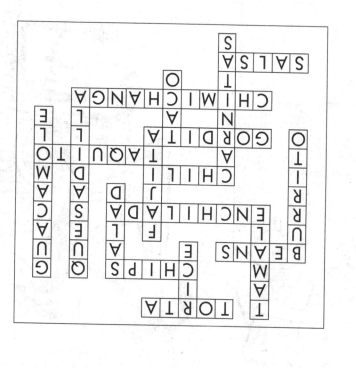

Busy Beavers

Compare these two pictures. Can you find at least **22** differences?

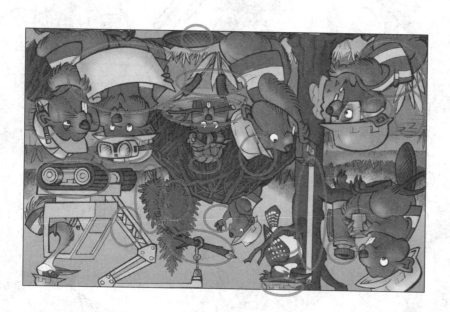

Daring Dara

Daring Dara is out on another adventure. This time she's rappelling down a sheer cliff.
What do you think she sees at the bottom? Draw it here.

Illustrated by Mike Moran

Inner Tubes

This hamster can't wait to chow down. But there is only one path that will lead him to his treats. Can you help him find it?

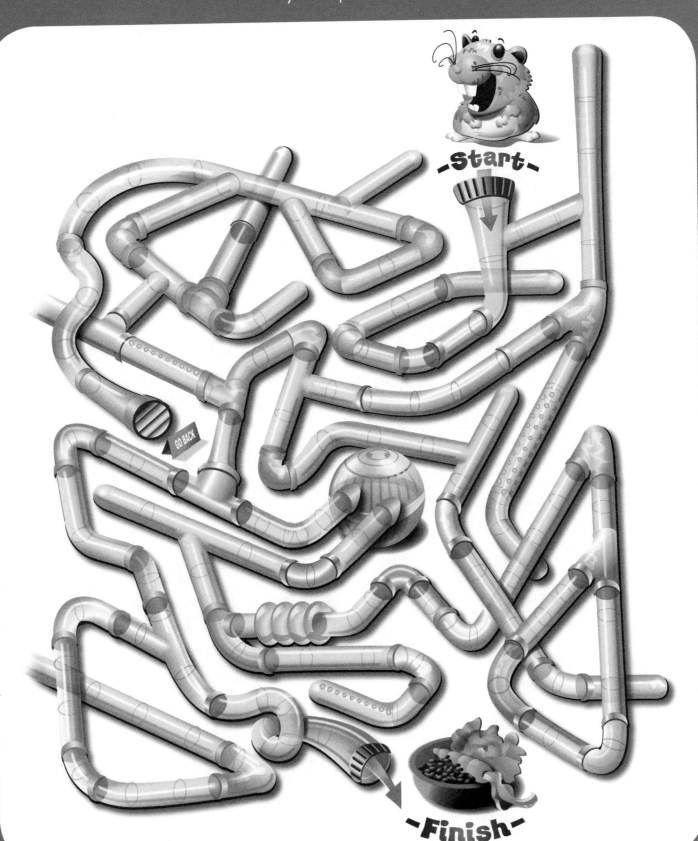

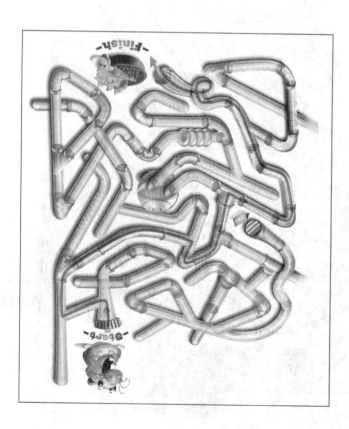

Word for Words

The letters in **SUBMARINE** can be used to make many other words. Use the clues below to come up with some of them. A flightless bird, for example, might make you think of the word EMU. See how many of the others you can guess.

S U B M A R I N E

1. **A flightless bird** <u>E M U</u>

2. **You might ride to school in this.** — — — —

3. **A male sheep** — — —

4. **Farm building** — — — — —

5. **Not far** — — — —

6. **Umbrella weather** — — — — —

7. **Horse hair** — — — —

8. **A flashlight ray** — — — — —

9. **Subtraction sign** — — — — — —

10. **Ambulance sound** — — — — —

11. **He or she works with a doctor.** — — — — — —

12. **1 is one.** — — — — — —

Illustrated by Wendy Wax

1. EMU
2. BUS
3. RAM
4. BARN
5. NEAR
6. RAIN
7. MANE
8. BEAM
9. MINUS
10. SIREN
11. NURSE
12. NUMBER

Tic Tac Ice Cream

What do the ice-cream cups in each row (horizontally, vertically, and diagonally) have in common?

Illustrated by Helena Bogosian

What flavor of ice cream do bikers like the least?
Rocky road.

What did the banana do when it heard the ice cream?
It split.

Where do you learn how to make ice cream?
Sundae school.

Brain Games

Take your brain on a hike. How far can you go?

START

Other than a faucet, **NAME SOMETHING THAT DRIPS.**

When you draw, would you rather have a **table** or a **rug** under your paper?

Which words are **TRICKY** for you to **SPELL?**

What's special about your favorite stuffed animal?

How is a sleeping bag different from a bed?

If you were making an **obstacle course** for your friends, **WHAT WOULD IT BE LIKE?**

In what ways are **SUMMER** and **WINTER** alike?

What materials were used to make **YOUR HOME?**

What would it be like if your school were in an amusement park?

How is your family like a sports team?

What can you do indoors when you have **LOTS OF ENERGY?**

THE END

Illustrated by Erin Mauterer

Cats and Dogs

Which **12** objects are exactly the same in these two pictures?

Illustrated by Kelly Kennedy

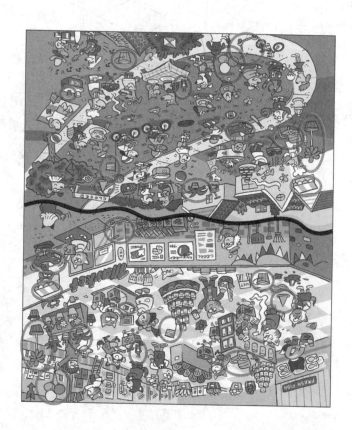

A Leap of Logic

It's time for the annual Lakeside County frog-jumping contest. Taylor and two of her friends have entered their frogs. Using the clues below, can you figure out whose frog is whose and what place each frog took in the contest?

Use the chart to keep track of your answers. Put an **X** in each box that can't be true and an **O** in boxes that match.

	Freddie	Spot	Hoppy	1st	2nd	3rd
Taylor						
Madison						
Cameron						

1. Taylor's frog finished after Hoppy.
2. Madison's frog finished before Cameron's frog and Spot.
3. Freddie finished second.

Taylor: Spot, 3rd place
Madison: Hoppy, 1st place
Cameron: Freddie, 2nd place

What's Wrong?

Which things in this picture are silly? It's up to you!

Illustrated by Kelly Kennedy

Just Sayin'...

Give the dentist something to say and the shark something to think.
Then find the hidden banana, baseball cap, book, magnifying glass, and sock.

Illustrated by David Coulson

Hidden Pictures®

Look at that rainbow peeking out from the clouds! Can you find the hidden objects in this scene?

Illustrated by Jackie Stafford

crescent moon

bowl

cupcake

envelope

button

fish

adhesive bandage

toucan

candle

toothbrush

banana

bell

kite

teacup

baseball bat

Grab a Chair

We've rounded up **21** kinds of chairs. They are hidden in the grid up, down, across, backwards, and diagonally. So pull up a seat and begin!

Word List

~~ADIRONDACK~~	DIRECTOR'S	OFFICE
BARREL	EASY	PATIO
BEACH	FOLDING	ROCKING
BEANBAG	HIGH	SWIVEL
BUTTERFLY	LADDERBACK	TULIP
CAPTAIN'S	LAWN	WINDSOR
CHESTERFIELD	LOUNGE	WING

```
Q B U T T E R F L Y K F H
D I R E C T O R S C K O E
R O S D N I W L A B N L H
K E G N U O L D A I I D M
C A P T A I N S L W O I B
A S T Y U O F E G F N N A
B Y W Q R L V R F W G G R
R Q C I X I I E W O H R
E R D Q W N C P H G I H E
D A T S I E A H S L T A L
D G S G N I K C O R A K A
A V R D G W L A Q L P H B
L D L E I F R E T S E H C
X S S B E A N B A G F A B
```

Q	B	U	T	T	E	R	F	L	Y	K	F	H
D	I	R	E	C	T	O	R	S	C	K	O	E
R	O	S	D	N	I	W	L	A	B	N	L	H
K	E	G	N	U	O	L	D	A	I	I	D	M
C	A	P	T	A	I	N	S	L	W	O	I	B
A	S	T	Y	U	O	F	E	G	F	N	N	A
B	Y	W	Q	R	L	V	R	F	W	G	G	R
R	Q	C	I	X	I	I	I	E	W	O	H	R
E	R	D	Q	W	N	C	P	H	G	I	H	E
D	A	T	S	I	E	A	H	S	L	T	A	L
D	G	S	G	N	I	K	C	O	R	A	K	A
A	V	R	D	G	W	L	A	Q	L	P	H	B
L	D	L	E	I	F	R	E	T	S	E	H	C
X	S	S	B	E	A	N	B	A	G	F	A	B

Dinnertime

Compare these two pictures. Can you find at least **14** differences?

Illustrated by Scott Angle

Rated L for Laughs

Nora and her friends give this movie two thumbs up—way up.
What do you think is making them laugh so hard?
Draw the movie scene you think they are watching.

Bull's-Eye

This parachuter is floating to Earth. Can you help him land safely right on target?

Illustrated by Jim Steck

Noteworthy

Reed found a secret note tucked in his desk during music class. Can you help him read it? To crack the code, first write down each letter that has a number *1* above it in order in the spaces below. Then do the same with number *2* letters, then number *3*, and so on, until you've filled in all the blanks.

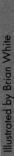

D E A R _ _ _ _ _ _,

_ _ _ _ _ _ _ _ _ _ _ _ _ _ _ _ _ _ _ _ _.

_ _

_ _ _ _ _ _ _ _ _ _ _ _ _ _ _ _!

_ _ _ _ _ _ _ _ _,

_ _ _ _ _ _ _

Dear Reed,
See you at band practice. Bring a ladder
so you can reach the high notes!
Your friend,
Melody

Tic Tac Butterfly

What do the butterflies in each row (horizontally, vertically, and diagonally) have in common?

Illustrated by Carlina Farias

Why did the boy throw butter out the window?
To see the butterfly.

What is a butterfly's favorite subject at school?
Mothematics.

Who is the king of the insects?
The monarch butterfly.

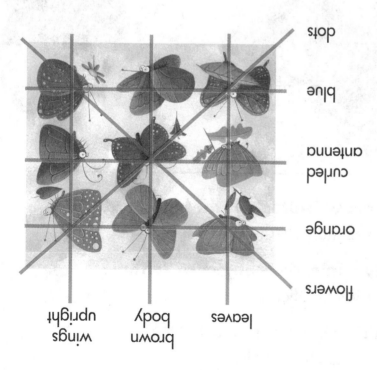

dots

blue

curled antenna

orange

flowers

wings upright

brown body

leaves

Brain Games

START HERE
Take your brain on a hike. How far can you go?

What is your favorite food to **eat in the winter?**

"Someone must be playing basketball outside," said Brandon. **What might make him think that?**

Name three different places where you would find a sticker.

How does a bicycle work?

For what activities do people use their ELBOWS a lot? What about their WRISTS? Their KNEES?

How do you let your family know HOW YOU FEEL?

When might people write to someone they don't know?

How do you think insects find their way around in **tall grass?**

If you could start a business tomorrow, WHAT WOULD IT BE?

Name something that has teeth but was NEVER ALIVE.

THE END

What might be in a salad that **CAN'T** be grown in a garden?

honey for Sale

HONEY

Illustrated by Erin Mauterer

What's for Lunch?

Customers are often puzzled by the menu at Doyle's Deli.
See if you can sound out each of today's specials.

BONUS!
How many numbered tickets can you find in the scene?

SANDWICHES:
Turkey wrap
Salami sub
Grilled cheese
Roast beef panini

SOUPS:
Clam chowder
Gumbo
Chicken noodle
Tomato

BONUS: There are seven tickets.

Hidden Words

There are six words (not pictures!) hidden in the scene below.
Can you find **COOL**, **CUT**, **MAN**, **SEE**, **SNOW**, and **TELL**?

Illustrated by Jackie Stafford

 **TONGUE TWISTERS**
Say each one three times fast!

I see icy ice skaters.
Silly snowmen make chilly children smile.
Travis told Terri to twirl.

What's Wrong?®

Which things in this picture are silly? It's up to you!

CAR WASH

REX

9.5

Illustrated by Mitch Mortimer

Step by Step

Follow the steps to draw a giraffe or draw one from your own head.

1.

2.

3.

4.

5.

Illustrated by Ron Zalme

Hidden Pictures®

Leslie is deciding between one scoop or two. Can you find the hidden objects in this scene?

Illustrated by Dave Klug

wedge of orange

pencil

football

fishhook

envelope

flower

comb

horseshoe

teacup

candle

artist's brush

hammer

golf club

sailboat

Grid Lock

Don't get locked out. Use the clues below to fill the grid.

Across ⇨ ⇨ ⇨ ⇨ ⇨

1. H₂O
4. Footwear
6. Measure of land
8. Chuckle; giggle
9. Abbreviation for "railroad"
10. Either ___
11. A room at the top of a house
13. To scrub clean
14. Current events
16. Used some money

Down ⬇ ⬇ ⬇ ⬇ ⬇

1. This comes from sheep.
2. ___ and fro
3. Wealthy
4. Like hay
5. Our planet
6. Once more
7. Makes money
11. Inquires
12. Penny
15. Myself

1 W	A	T	E	R

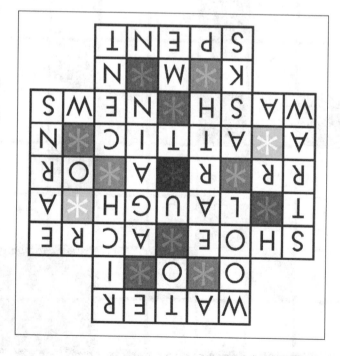

Supersized Salad

Compare these two pictures. Can you find at least **18** differences?

Illustrated by Pat Lewis

One Dark and Stormy Night

At last! Doctor Deviso's greatest experiment is finished.
Is it a scary dinosaur-poodle combination or a peanut butter, liverwurst, and pickle sandwich?
Use your imagination to draw what Dr. D. has been working on.

Illustrated by Mike Moran

F-ANT-astic Fun

The **Ant**-Farm Hoedown is getting started, but **Ant**hony, Sam**ant**ha, and Gr**ant** have just finished the spring pl**ant**ing and are running late. Can you get each of them to the party?

BONUS!
Find three pairs of pants that appear twice. Then find at least three objects with names that contain the word **ant**.

Illustrated by Pat Lewis

BONUS: fire hydrant, plants, and lantern.

What's the Meaning of This?

Each of these clues will lead you to a word or a phrase. You just have to look at them in the right way. For example, the first one might make you think of "Reading between the lines." Can you figure out the rest?

1

READING

2 JACK

3

P   P

4 BAN   ANA

5

somewhere

6 WONaDlEiRcLeAND

7 FUSS
nothing

8 PRAIRIE

9 FOOT

Puzzle by Denise Stanley

Illustrated by Hey Kids!

1. Reading between the lines
2. Jack-in-the-box
3. Two peas in a pod
4. Banana split
5. Somewhere over the rainbow
6. *Alice in Wonderland*
7. Big fuss over nothing
8. *Little House on the Prairie*
9. Bigfoot

Tic Tac Dog

What do the dogs in each row (horizontally, vertically, and diagonally) have in common?

Illustrated by Jennifer Morris

What is a dog's least favorite place to shop?
The flea market.

Which bones do dogs not like?
Trombones.

What dog loves to take bubble baths?
A shampoodle.

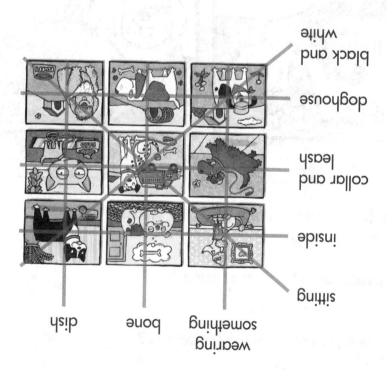

black and
white

doghouse

collar and
leash

inside

sitting

dish

bone

wearing
something

Brain Games

Take your brain on a hike. How far can you go?

START

What is your favorite number? Why?

What would it be like to sing whatever you wanted to say for a whole day?

WHAT COULD YOU USE TO WRITE ON A BALLOON?

If you were a bird, would you rather live in **a castle or a garden?** Why?

Name some things that come in a bag.

Do you eat the same foods when you go out as you eat at home? Why?

Which things around you right now are special or important to you?

How can different species communicate with each other?

What five qualities should a best friend have?

THE END

Who laughs with you the most?

WHAT TOOLS DO YOU KNOW HOW TO USE?

Illustrated by Erin Mauterer

Rhyme Time

In downtown Sillyville, there's a shawl on a ball, a pig in a wig, and a very wet pet!
What other rhyming things do you see?

Illustrated by Kelly Kennedy

We found these rhymes. You may have found others! bread/bed, mule/tool, goat/boat, bees/trees, red/shed, blue/shoe/glue, bird/ third, cone/stone, bite/kite, cook/ book, butterfly/pie, aardvark/dark, phone/bone, cat/mat, tie/good-bye/dragonfly, flag/ bag, fox/socks/mailbox, duck/ truck, star/car, toad/road, dog/log, bandstand/sand, wrench/ bench, hen/pen, raccoon/spoon, croc/clock, boar/door, cat/hat, showers/flowers

Game On!

Andrew and three of his friends entered a video game competition. From the clues below, can you figure out which game each friend played and which place he or she took?

Use the chart to keep track of your answers. Put an **X** in each box that can't be true and an **O** in boxes that match.

	Space Travel	Golf Guru	Race Car Fun	Zany Zoo	1st	2nd	3rd	4th
Andrew								
Briana								
Cassie								
Diego								

1. One of the girls took 1st place in Zany Zoo.

2. Andrew's game had exactly 8 letters in its name.

3. Diego's place was ahead of Briana, but behind Andrew.

4. Briana played her favorite game, Race Car Fun.

Andrew: Golf Guru, 2nd
Briana: Race Car Fun, 4th
Cassie: Zany Zoo, 1st
Diego: Space Traveler, 3rd

What's Wrong?®

Which things in this picture are silly? It's up to you!

Just Sayin'...

Give these tightrope walkers something to say. Then find the hidden baseball ball, crescent moon, doughnut, fish, and slice of pizza.

Illustrated by Dave Clegg

Hidden Pictures®

Brandon is taking a closer look under the microscope. Can you find the hidden objects in this scene?

Illustrated by Jackie Stafford

tack

crescent moon

artist's brush

banana

slice of pizza

shoe

sock

ruler

star

baseball

hammer

fish

teacup

bell

toothbrush

Icky Ice Cream

This wacky dessert menu includes **20** of the grossest ice-cream flavors in the world! Can you find them all? They are hidden up, down, across, backwards, and diagonally. Only the words in CAPITAL letters are hidden. When you're done, write the leftover letters in order in the spaces below. Go from left to right and top to bottom. They will spell out the secret flavor.

Menu

Almond ~~ASPARAGUS~~
Banana BUG
Chocolate CHEESE
CRAB Cream
DANDELION Delight
Frozen FUNGUS
Fudge FISH
Grapefruit GRUEL
Heavenly HOT DOG
Lime LIVERS
MEAT Medley
Orange OCTOPUS
Peanut Butter PORK
Peppermint BAT
Rocky RODENT
SEAWEED surprise
SOUR Cookie Dough
SQUID-elicious
Tasty TOMATO
TROUT Trifle

The secret flavor is

__ __ __ __ __ __ __ __ __ __ __ __ !

Illustrated by Mike Moran

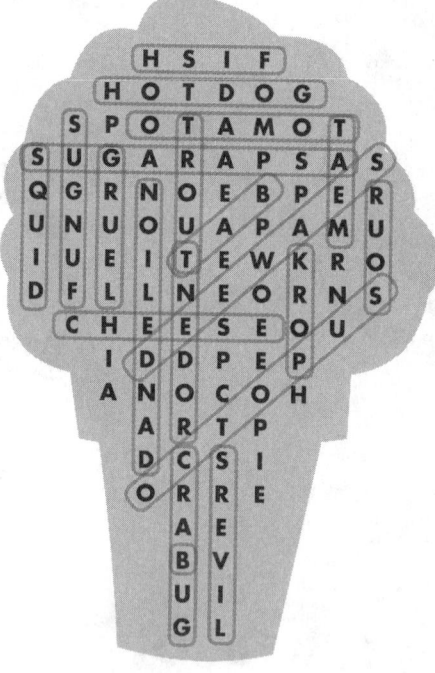

The secret Puzzlemania flavor is
PEPPERONI PEACH PIE!

Barnyard High Jinks

Compare these two pictures. Can you find at least **19** differences?

Illustrated by Kevin Zimmer

Past Time

Taylor built a time machine and threw it into reverse.
She's gone back in time, but to where? Does she see knights or cave people?
Dinosaurs or Vikings? Use your imagination to show when and where she landed.

Straw Twister

Everyone's enjoying an ice-cream soda.
But who is drinking which one? Follow each straw to find out!

It's Black and White

Unscramble each of the words below to get the name of something that is usually black and white. Then write each numbered letter in its correct space to see the answer to the riddle.

1. CEDI   <u>D</u> <u>I</u> <u>C</u> <u>E</u>
                          11

2. BRAZE   __ __ __ __ __
           6

3. ADNAP   __ __ __ __ __
         8

4. NUSKK   __ __ __ __ __
               3

5. NINEPUG   __ __ __ __ __ __ __
          10

6. ANIOP SKYE   __ __ __ __ __ __ __ __ __
                   4   7

7. ICELOP ARC   __ __ __ __ __ __ __ __ __
             5

8. CREOCS LABL   __ __ __ __ __ __ __ __ __
                  12   1

9. RELLIK LAWHE   __ __ __ __ __ __ __ __ __ __
                        9

10. SCRODROWS   __ __ __ __ __ __ __ __ __
             2

What is black and white and sleeps a lot?

__ __ __ __ __ __ __ - __ __ __ <u>E</u> __ !
1 2 3 4 5 6 7   8 9 10 11 12

What is black and white and sleeps a lot?
A SNOOZE-PAPER!

1. DICE
2. ZEBRA
3. PANDA
4. SKUNK
5. PENGUIN
6. PIANO KEYS
7. POLICE CAR
8. SOCCER BALL
9. KILLER WHALE
10. CROSSWORD

Tic Tac Sandwich

What do the sandwiches in each row (horizontally, vertically, and diagonally) have in common?

What's a skunk's favorite sandwich?
Peanut butter and smelly.

What's a bear's favorite sandwich?
Growled cheese.

What's a ghost's favorite sandwich?
Booloney.

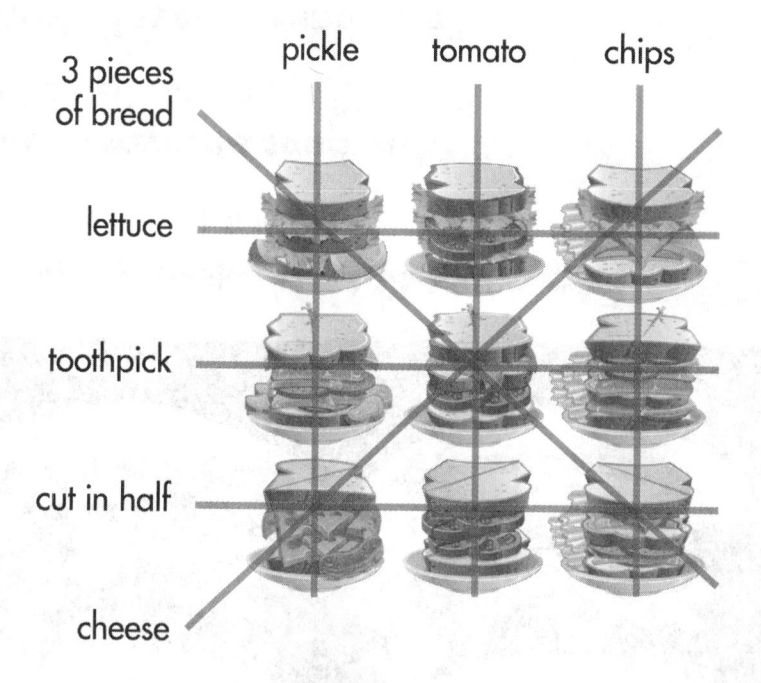

Brain Games

START HERE
Take your brain on a hike.
How far can you go?

Who is **THE BEST** at making you laugh?

What do you do to cool off when you **FEEL HOT?**

Can you list some **SOUNDS** that can be **MISTAKEN** for each other?

Which are you?
Intelligent?
Energetic?
Artistic?
Athletic?
Can you choose which traits you have?

Name something in your home that feels . . .

PRICKLY!

SMOOTH!

BUMPY!

The Problem with **NOT** Being Scared of Monsters
Dan Richards
Illustrated by Robert Neubecker

Which gets your attention first: a book's **title,** **author,** or **cover?**

Which do you like better **GLOVES** or **MITTENS?** Why?

Do you like all **SHADES** of your favorite color?

INSTEAD OF SCISSORS, what might an animal use to cut things?

Which sports are easy to play **when it's windy?**

THE END

What is the **best smell?** Why?

Illustrated by Erin Mauterer

Snail Shopping

Xu's favorite pet store is a little unusual. The two elevators stop only on certain floors, and the caterpillars keep escaping from their habitat! Find the **15** caterpillars. Then figure out how many times Xu had to change elevators to complete his to-do list in order.

XU'S TO-DO'S

1. Buy pet snail.   2. Have snail groomed.   3. Go to gastropod obedience class.
4. Buy *Snail Without Fail* book.   5. Grab a seaweed-mushroom smoothie.   6. Take photo with new friend!

Xu changed elevators four times. After riding the orange elevator to floor 5, Xu returned to the ground floor to change to the blue elevator. He rode the blue elevator to floors 4 and then 2, changed to orange for floor 3, changed to blue for floor 6, and changed to orange for floor 7.

Hidden Words

There are six words (not pictures!) hidden at the pool.
Can you find **COOL**, **DIVE**, **HOT**, **SPLASH**, **SUNSCREEN**, and **WATER**?

Illustrated by Kelly Kennedy

 ## TONGUE TWISTERS
Say each one three times fast!

Sally always shares sunscreen.
Doug doesn't dive unless it's deep.
Walter whistled wildly in the water.

What's Wrong?

Which things in this picture are silly? It's up to you!

Illustrated by Chuck Dillon

Step by Step

Follow the steps to draw a *Tyrannosaurus rex* or draw one from your own head.

Illustrated by Ron Zalme

Hidden Pictures®

It's the perfect night for a pizza dinner. Can you find the hidden objects in this scene?

Illustrated by Dave Klug

horseshoe

hammer

flower

envelope

fishhook

football

candle

sailboat

pencil

artist's brush

comb

wedge of orange

teacup

golf club

Candy Counter

No need to sugarcoat it, this is a sweet puzzle! Each of these candy names will fit into the grid in just one way. Use a word's length as a clue for where to put it. When you've filled them all in, write the letters in the shaded boxes in order in the spaces below to see the answer to the riddle.

What crop does a farmer with a sweet tooth grow?

Word List

GUM	LICORICE
~~MINT~~	LOLLIPOP
FUDGE	CANDY CANE
TAFFY	JELLY BEAN
CARAMEL	CHOCOLATE BAR
TRUFFLE	PEANUT BRITTLE

What crop does a farmer
with a sweet tooth grow?
CANDY CORN

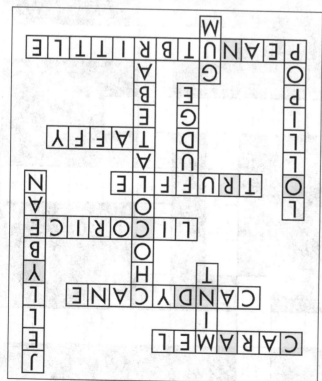

Dance with Me

Compare these two pictures. Can you find at least **12** differences?

The Sky's the Limit

These kids see something surprising in the sky!
Draw what you think they are looking at.

Illustrated by Mike Moran

Penguin Path

This penguin is hungry! Can you help him slip and slide down a path that leads into the water so he can fish for food? Be careful not to crash into any other penguins.

Start

Finish

Sudoku Garden

Each of these grids holds a garden made up of just one type of flower. Fill in the boxes so that each row, column, and six-letter section contains the letters of that flower. We've filled in some of the letters to get you started. Can you fill in the rest?

VIOLET

V	O	I	L	E	T
	L	E		I	O
	V			T	E
O	E		I		
	V	E	O		I
E	I			L	

ORCHID

H	D	C	O	R	I
		R	D		
	H	I		O	D
		D		H	R
C				D	O
	R	O	H	I	

CLOVER

E	R	O	L	V	C
V		L			
			O		V
O			C		
R	V		E		O
L	O	E		C	R

Illustrated by Terry Taylor   Puzzle by Renee Heiss

CLOVER

ORCHID

VIOLET

Tic Tac Insect

What do the insects in each row (horizontally, vertically, and diagonally) have in common?

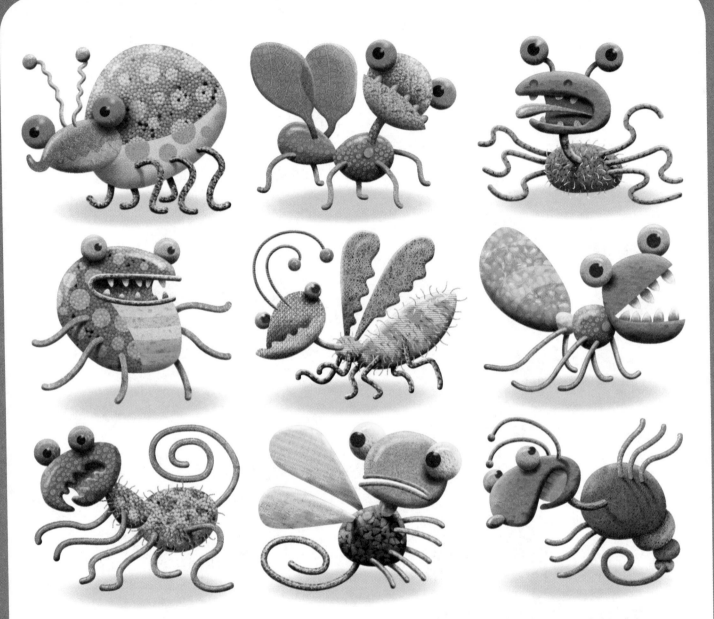

Illustrated by Paul Richer

What kind of bug tells time?
A clockroach.

Why did the fly fly?
Because the spider spied her.

What is a bug's least favorite vegetable?
Squash.

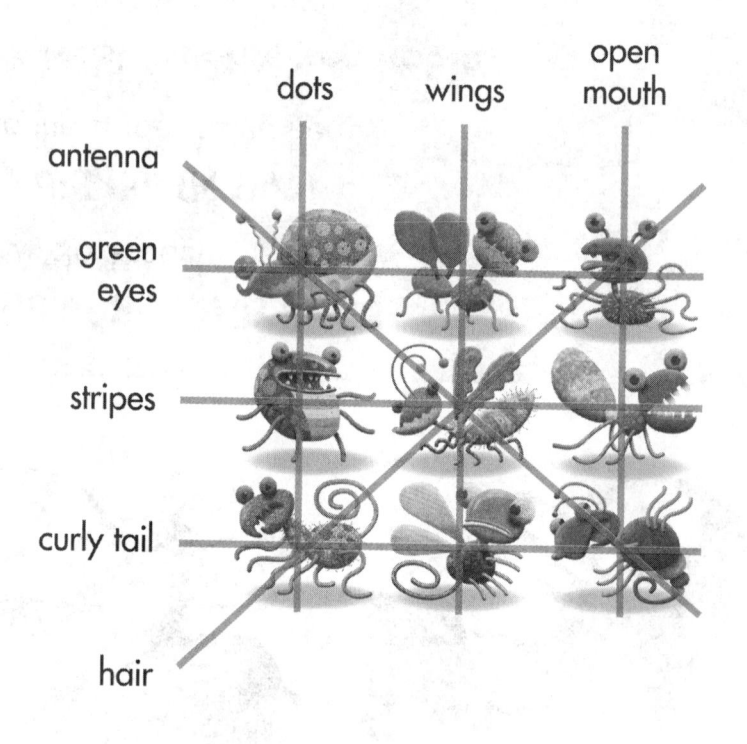

Rhyming Replacements

In this scene, at least **10** items have been replaced by a rhyming item. For example, a candle has been replaced by a sandal. How many replacements can you spot?

Illustrated by Chuck Dillon

We found these rhyming replacements. You may have found others! owl for towel, moon for spoon, skate for plate, shower for flower, frog for dog, sandal for candle, kite for light, bear for pear, fan for pan, 3 for tree, hare for chair, car for jar, and rope for soap

The Plot Thickens

Jack and three friends are sharing a plot in their community garden this summer. From the clues below, can you figure out which friend planted what type of veggie and what kind of flower?

Use the chart to keep track of your answers. Put an **X** in each box that can't be true and an **O** in boxes that match.

	Peas	Corn	Squash	Lettuce	Sunflowers	Marigolds	Petunias	Zinnias
Jack								
Lily								
Garrett								
Rosemary								

1. Lily's vegetable and flower start with consecutive letters of the alphabet.
2. Jack does not like corn.
3. Rosemary's veggie and flower start with the same letter.
4. Garrett planted his favorite flowers, petunias.

Puzzle by Karen Smith

Jack: peas and zinnias
Lily: lettuce and marigolds
Garrett: corn and petunias
Rosemary: squash and sunflowers

What's Wrong?

Which things in this picture are silly? It's up to you!

Illustrated by Mike Dammer

Just Sayin'...

Give this elephant something to say. Then find the hidden balloon, glove, slice of pizza, spool of thread, and star.

Hidden Pictures®

After a full day of skiing, everyone warms up by the fire. Can you find the hidden objects in this scene?

Illustrated by Iryna Bodnaruk

plunger · pennant · ice-cream cone · feather duster · crown · boomerang · open book

rolling pin · mallet · ball · dustpan · horseshoe · butter knife · pencil

Easy as Pie!

Seventeen types of pie are baked into this grid. They are hidden up, down, across, backwards, and diagonally. Go ahead and dig in!

```
        C O C O N U T
    Y I C E C R E A M
    Y P M I N C E M E A T
  U O E P R U N E W H I P R
  T U A Y E L E M O N C E T B
H C R N R E Q B N A P E A R B
Q H T U R T R K E Y L I M E P
Y E E T E A M Y     N A C E P
U R E B B L P L         E O
M R T U Q O U F           S
Y H T A C M O
R A T P O P O T
H E P H K H B
  R L C I S L
  E A N E X
```

Word List

- ~~APPLE~~
- **BERRY**
- **CHERRY**
- **CHOCOLATE**
- **COCONUT**
- **ICE CREAM**
- **KEY LIME**
- **LEMON**
- **MINCEMEAT**
- **PEACH**
- **PEANUT BUTTER**
- **PEAR**
- **PECAN**
- **PRUNE WHIP**
- **PUMPKIN**
- **RHUBARB**
- **SHOOFLY**

Bonus Puzzle

When you've circled all the words, we've got an extra treat for you. The answer to the riddle below is hidden in a row or column. See if you can find it.

What's the best thing to put in a pie?

Y _ _ _ _ _ _ _ _ _ _ _ !

Puzzle by Stacey Williams

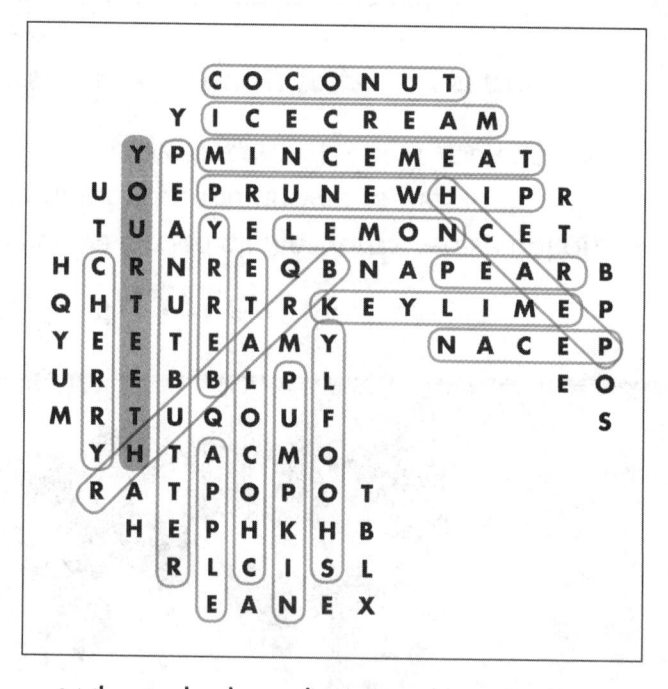

What's the best thing to put in a pie?
YOUR TEETH

Planetary Parade

Compare these two pictures. Can you find at least **20** differences?

Illustrated by Scott Angle

Sea This

The world-famous marine biologist, Dr. Kelp, has stumbled upon something exciting on her dive. What do you think she found? Draw it here.

Maize Maze

Find the quickest path through the corn maze from ENTER to EXIT. Then find a path that goes through every flagged checkpoint. Can you also find a path that goes through only even-numbered checkpoints?

BONUS!
Tom completed the maze and collected a letter sticker at each checkpoint. Can you help him unscramble the letters to answer the riddle?

Name: Tom

COLONEL SHUCK'S
CORN MAZE WORD SCRAMBLE

F D O C L E I N R

What has thousands of ears but can't hear?

A _ _ _ _ _ _ _ _ _

Illustrated by Pat Lewis

BONUS: A CORNFIELD.

Fun on the Sun

Can you shed some light on this puzzle? To find the answer to the riddle below, first cross out all the pairs of matching letters. Then write the remaining letters in order in the spaces beneath the riddle.

SS   BB   LL   IM   QQ   CC   TT
VE   DD   XX   EE   OO   RY   JJ
NN   WW   II   PL   ZZ   AA   KK
UU   EA   SS   LL   HH   OO   SE
RR   DD   DT   VV   EE   II   MM
YY   UU   OO   OH   PP   CC   EA
GG   TT   TY   AA   KK   OU   EE

What did the sun say when it was introduced to Earth?

'_ _ _ _ _
_ _ _ _ _ _ _
_ _ _ _ _ _ .

Illustrated by Dave Clegg

What did the sun say when it was
introduced to Earth?
"I'M VERY PLEASED TO HEAT YOU."

Tic Tac Frog

What do the frogs in each row (horizontally, vertically, and diagonally) have in common?

Where do funny frogs sit?
On silly pads.

What happened to the frog that parked illegally?
He got toad.

Why are frogs always happy?
Because they eat whatever bugs them.

Illustrated by Carolina Farias

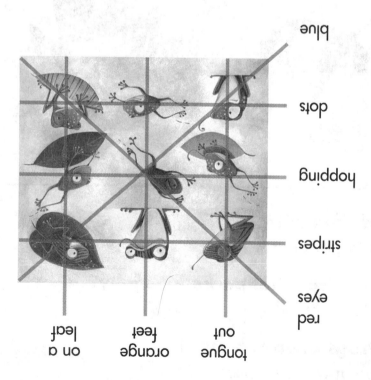

blue

dots

hopping

stripes

red
eyes

tongue
out

orange
feet

on a
leaf

Brain Games

START HERE

Take your brain on a hike. How far can you go?

Name something you see on license plates.

What do these foods have in common?

KETCHUP

MAYONNAISE

RELISH

Name 3 things a great vacation spot should have.

What would you like to wear on a T-shirt?

Tell about a time when you learned from a mistake.

Josh got sunburn on just ONE ARM. How could that happen?

How is a poem different from a song?

What makes a cracking sound?

What would make a good suitcase for a mouse?

How do people decide on a hairstyle?

Which do you think would bounce better on a trampoline, a **PERSON** or a **WATER BALLOON?** Why?

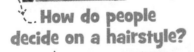

"The days are getting longer," said Tara. What did she mean?

THE END

Illustrated by Erin Mauterer

Rush-Hour Rhymes

It's rush hour—but take all the time you need to find: two matching dresses, plants, and lizards; a toad being towed; a moose eating mousse; and a sail for sale.

BONUS!
Find these hidden objects:
pink purse, red magnet,
white candle, light gray cane
and flowerpot, and dark
gray shoe.

Illustrated by Mary Sullivan

Hidden Words

There are six words (not pictures!) hidden in the scene below.
Can you find **BRUSH**, **BUCKET**, **COLOR**, **PAINT**, **ROLLER**, and **TARP**?

Illustrated by Kelly Kennedy

 ## TONGUE TWISTERS
Say each one three times fast!

Patches picked the purple paint.
Trevor tried not to trip on the tarp.
Rachel reached with her roller.

What's Wrong?®

Which things in this picture are silly? It's up to you!

Illustrated by Chuck Dillon

Step by Step

Follow the steps to draw a horse or draw one from your own head.

1.

2.

3.

4.

5.

Hidden Pictures®

These circus performers love hearing the crowd cheer. Can you find the hidden objects in this scene?

Illustrated by Jackie Stafford

butterfly

crown

ring

candle

open book

golf club

crescent moon

heart

crayon

slice of pizza

ice-cream cone

shoe

ax

tack

teacup

Aloha!

Howdy! Fourteen ways to say hello from around the world are listed here. Each greeting will fit into the grid in just one way. Use the number of letters in a greeting to help figure out where it will fit. Only the words in capital letters go in the grid.

Word List

BONJOUR (French)
~~CIAO~~ **(Italian)**
G'DAY (Australian)
GOD DAG (Swedish)
GUTEN TAG (German)
HOLA (Spanish)
JAMBO (Swahili)
KONNICHI WA
    (Japanese)
NAMASTE (Hindi)
NI HAO (Cantonese)
SALAAM (Arabic)
SHALOM (Hebrew)
WITAJ (Polish)
YIA SAS (Greek)

Illustrated by Dave Clegg

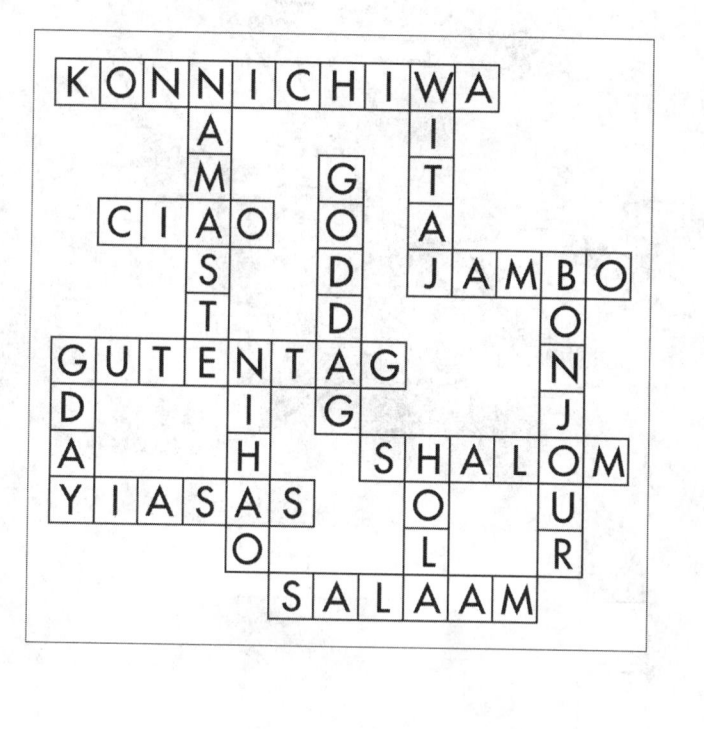

Rough Rapids

Compare these two pictures. Can you find at least **19** differences?

Illustrated by Mike DeSantis

Designer Clothes

Here's a brand-new T-shirt just for you. But you'll need to design it.
Will your shirt have words or pictures, or both? Will it be funny or fancy?
Use your imagination to create the T-shirt you've always wanted.

Illustrated by Mike Moran

Meet the Beetles

Mingo is meeting up with his friends. They've all made it to the middle of the maze. Can you help Mingo find his way there?

Illustrated by Mattia Cerato

Scrambled Space

Unscramble these space words. Once you have them all straightened out, read down the column of boxes to learn the answer to this riddle:

What do you get when you cross a galaxy and a toad?

RAMS — M A R [S]

METCO — _ _ _ _ [ ]

UNRATS — _ [ ] _ _ _ _

RITBO — _ _ [ ] _ _

LYMIK YAW — _ _ [ ] _ _ _ _ _

CLABK LOEH — _ _ _ [ ] _ _ _ _

TIPJUER — _ _ _ _ _ [ ] _

DREATSIO — _ _ _ _ [ ] _ _

SNUVE — _ _ _ _ [ ]

RAMS	MARS
METCO	COMET
UNRATS	SATURN
RITBO	ORBIT
LYMIK YAW	MILKY WAY
CLABK LOEH	BLACK HOLE
TIPJUER	JUPITER
DREATSIO	ASTEROID
SNUVE	VENUS

What do you get when you cross
a galaxy and a toad?
STAR WARTS

Tic Tac Bump

What do the bumper cars in each row (horizontally, vertically, and diagonally) have in common?

Illustrated by Scott Angle

What is a polar bear's favorite ride at the amusement park?
The polar coaster.

What do monsters ride on at the amusement park?
The scary-go-round.

Knock, knock.
Who's there?
Ice cream.
Ice cream who?
Ice cream on fast rides—
     don't you?

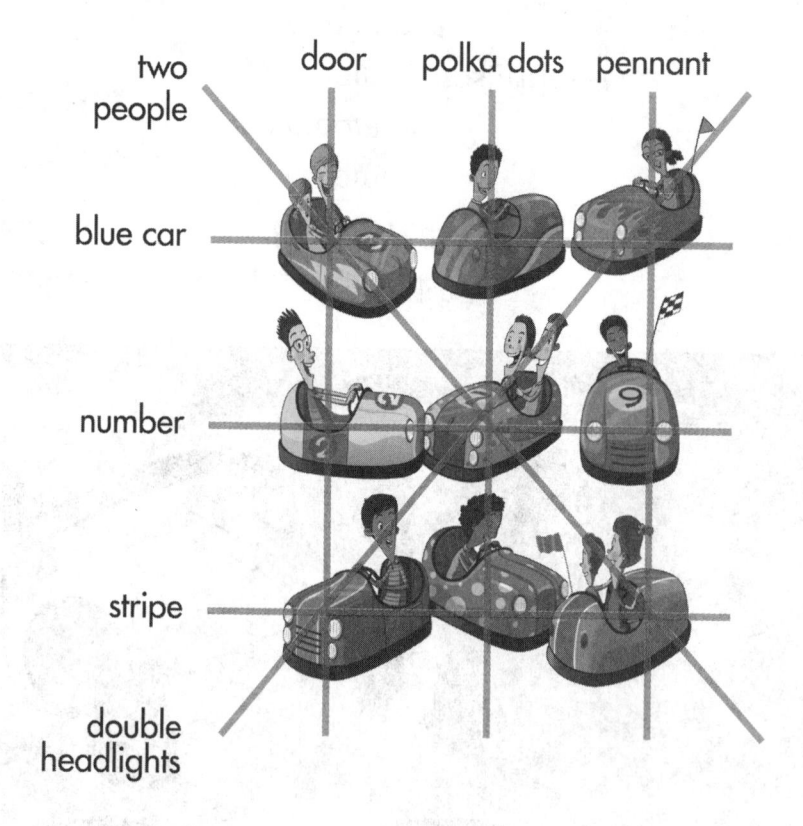

Brain Games

START HERE

Take your brain on a hike. How far can you go?

If you could rename your favorite color, what would you call it?

"Here's a little reward for all your hard work!" What might the reward be?

Which are you likely to do today? Wash, snack, buckle, fish, pedal, fly, comb, paint, spin.

Name some things that have roots.

From morning to evening, how does the view out your window change?

Would you rather be a little warm OR a little cool? Why?

How could you describe different shapes to someone without drawing them?

If Thanksgiving were in July, would your family eat different foods?

What can an octopus do that you can do, too?

How can you tell that someone wants to be friends?

THE END

If you were on a game show, would you rather compete by yourself or as part of a team? Why?

Name something with an inside that's very different from its outside.

Illustrated by Erin Mauterer

Plane Puzzler

Planes are about to take off from this airport—but where are they going? Sound out each U.S. city name on the sign. Then find the passenger who's going there by unscrambling the state names on the suitcases.

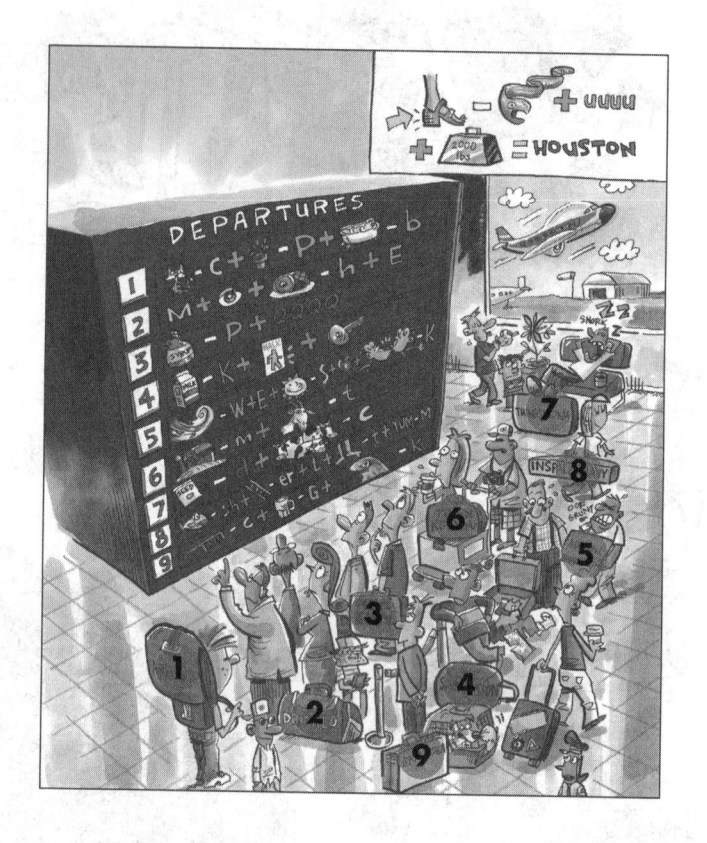

1. Atlanta, Georgia
2. Miami, Florida
3. Syracuse, New York
4. Milwaukee, Wisconsin
5. Indianapolis, Indiana
6. Fargo, North Dakota
7. Seattle, Washington
8. Philadelphia, Pennsylvania
9. Omaha, Nebraska

Each of these clues will lead you to a word or a phrase. You just have to look at them in the right way. For example, the first one might make you think of "One in a million." Can you figure out the rest?

1 MILLI**1**ON

2 ME REPEAT

3 WEAR / LONG

4 CA just SE

5 HEAD / HEELS

6 DANCE DANCE DANCE DANCE DANCE DANCE *

7

8 ROADS / ROADS

1. One in a million
2. Repeat after me
3. Long underwear
4. Just in case
5. Head over heels
6. Square dance
7. Hole in one
8. Crossroads

What's Wrong?

Which things in this picture are silly? It's up to you!

Illustrated by James Yamasaki

Just Sayin'...

Give this superhero something to say. Then find the hidden
apple, domino, doughnut, football, open book, and ruler.

Hidden Pictures®

Someone needs to clean his room! Can you find the hidden objects in this scene?

Illustrated by Kelly Kennedy

pen

wedge of cheese

saw

light bulb

pie

shovel

coin

magnifying glass

telescope

nail

spoon

lock

pine tree

pennant

All Talk

We've hidden **20** ways to say something in this grid. They are hiding up, down, across, backwards, and diagonally. How many can you find?

Word List

~~BABBLE~~
BELLOW
BLATHER
CRY
EXCLAIM
HISS
HOLLER
JABBER
MUMBLE
MURMUR

PRATTLE
PROCLAIM
RAMBLE
SCREAM
SCREECH
SHRIEK
SPEAK
WHISPER
WHOOP
YELL

```
S P E A K E T R E E E I C
Z M U M B L E L L Y W S
S H H E D T X B B E O H
G Y H X W T B V M L L H
P R O C L A I M A L L H
H S L L B R S H R I E K
C C L A A P R M W W B B
E R E I B L A T H E R M
E E R M S H H O I C N C
R A M Q H Z O F S O R D
C M W I Q P V O P I S Y
S E S M J A B B E R H G
M S R U M R U M R E H D
```

Illustrated by Scott Angle

Puzzle by Charlotte Gunnufson

```
S P E A K E T R E E I C
Z M U M B L E L L Y W C S
S H H E D T X B B E O S H
G Y H X W T T B V M L L H H
P R O C L A I M A L L H H
H S L L B R S H R I E K
C C L A A P R M W W B B
E R I B L A T H E R M
E E I M S H H O I C N C
R A M Q H Z O F S O R D
C M W I Q P V O P I S Y
S E S M J A B B E R H G
M S R U M R U M R E H D
```

Dapper Dogs

Compare these two pictures. Can you find at least **21** differences?

Illustrated by Jackie Stafford

Raise the Flag

Fiona is forming her own country! Now she needs a flag.
What do you think her country's flag should look like?
Design it here.

Illustrated by Mike Moran

Pencil Paths

Which pencil wrote each word?

Hidden Pairs

Each pair of words below is hiding something. Look closely and you'll find a pair of shorter but related words in the original pair. For example, in the first pair you can find **on** and **off**. Can you spot the other hidden pairs?

1. s**on**g, c**off**ee

2. grouping, landowner

3. haunted, unclear

4. thighbone, mayflower

5. holiday, knighthood

6. shortcut, totally

7. photograph, scolded

8. hammerhead, snail

9. merchandise, barefooted

10. fishbowl, sparrow

11. architect, admission

12. refunded, ballgames

Illustrated by Dan McGeehan

1. on, off
2. up, down
3. aunt, uncle
4. high, low
5. day, night
6. short, tall
7. hot, cold
8. hammer, nail
9. hand, foot
10. bow, arrow
11. hit, miss
12. fun, games

Tic Tac Lunch

What do the lunch carriers in each row (horizontally, vertically, and diagonally) have in common?

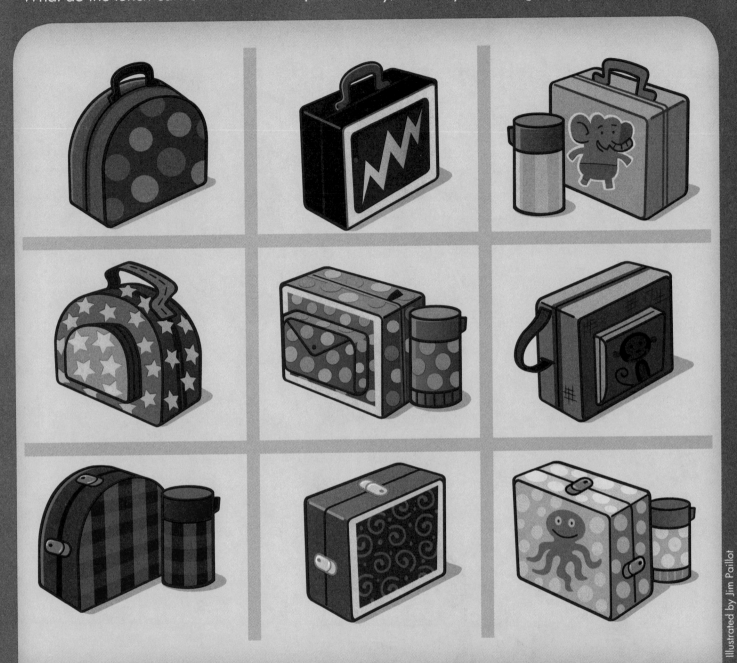

Illustrated by Jim Paillot

Where do comedians go for lunch?
The laugh-eteria.

How do you ask a dinosaur to lunch?
"Tea, Rex?"

What did the clock do after eating lunch?
It went back four seconds.

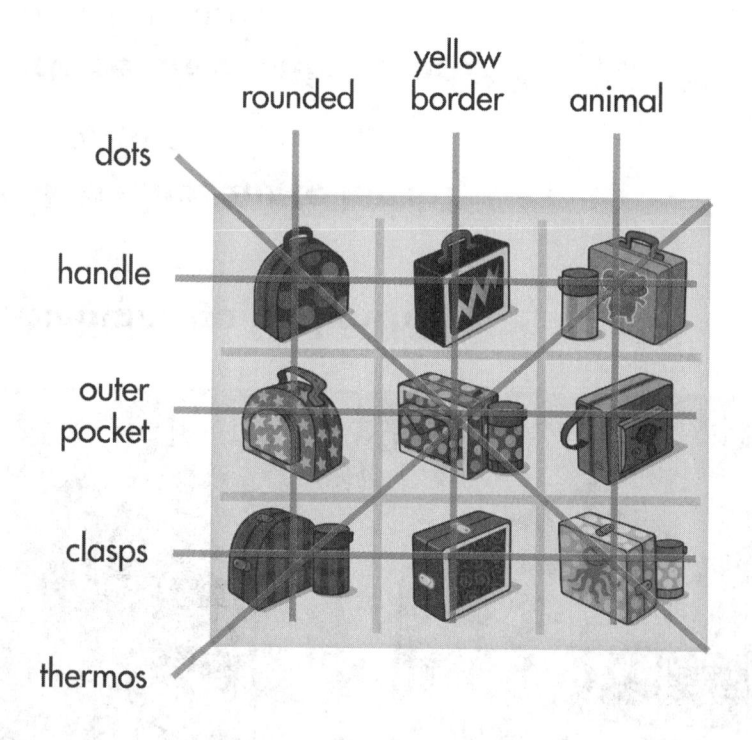

Brain Games

START HERE

Take your brain on a hike. How far can you go?

Would you rather WALK or DANCE?

If you made lunch for your family, **what would you serve?**

What was the first thing you said this morning?

Could a sink be made from STONE? Could a *BED*? A *SLED*? A *FLAG*?

Which fruits would be EASIEST TO JUGGLE? Which would be hardest?

Could **scissors** be used to slice **A CAKE?**

Name five things you do every evening.

What would your **SUPERHERO NAME be?**

What helps you keep trying when the going **GETS TOUGH?**

What could you make a ball of clay into, without flattening the ball?

THE END

Can you balance on one foot? **On your HEEL? On your TOES?**

Name some things you can twirl.

Illustrated by Erin Mauterer